Gifted To:

From:

Date:

RESCUE PRAYERS

FOR A DIFFICULT DIAGNOSIS

---

30 Days of Prayer for
Times of Crisis

Copyright © 2024, Rescue Prayers

All rights reserved. To copy or duplicate any portion of this book, please contact the publisher.

www.rescueprayers.com

PO Box 1264
Warrenton, VA 20188

HB ISBN: 978-1-963701-20-3

Cover Design: Michelle Lenger
Cover Image: © iStock
Interior Images: © Shutterstock

"Commit your cause to the Lord; let him deliver—
let him rescue the one in whom he delights!"

PSALM 22:8 (NRSV)

Table of Contents

Introduction: How to Use Rescue Prayers ix

Day 1	Prayer for Facing a Difficult Diagnosis	1
Day 2	Prayer for Choosing the Right Treatment	5
Day 3	Prayer for Provision for Financial Burdens	9
Day 4	Prayer for Navigating Challenges at Work	13
Day 5	Prayer for Relief from Physical Pain	17
Day 6	Prayer for Improved Quality of Life	21
Day 7	Prayer for Fears About Death	25
Day 8	Prayer for Emotional Well-Being	29
Day 9	Prayer for My Family and Relationships	33
Day 10	Prayer for Those Caring for Me	37
Day 11	Prayer for Strength Navigating Loss of Independence	41
Day 12	Prayer for Finding the Right Care	45
Day 13	Prayer for Wisdom in Medical Decisions	49
Day 14	Prayer for Accepting Changes to Future Plans	53
Day 15	Prayer for My Changing Physical Appearance	57
Day 16	Prayer for Establishing Healthy Coping Methods	61

Day 17	Prayer for Guidance Managing My Medications	65
Day 18	Prayer for Protection for My Children	69
Day 19	Prayer for Spiritual Strength Amid Doubt	73
Day 20	Prayer for Calm in Loss of Control	77
Day 21	Prayer for Comfort in Isolation and Loneliness	81
Day 22	Prayer for Release from Guilt and Shame	85
Day 23	Prayer for Rest on Sleepless Nights	89
Day 24	Prayer for Mental Clarity and Focus	93
Day 25	Prayer for Restoration of Relational Intimacy	97
Day 26	Prayer for Provision of Reliable Transportation	101
Day 27	Prayer for Help with Nutritional Changes	105
Day 28	Prayer for Guidance for Alternative Therapies	109
Day 29	Prayer for Faith Amid Doubt and Uncertainty	113
Day 30	Prayer for Miraculous Intervention and Healing	117

INTRODUCTION
How to Use Rescue Prayers

Dear One,

There have been many times in my life when I encountered devastating situations that seemed impossible to handle—or even to process. In deep distress, I wept, begged, demanded, pleaded, and called on the Lord to intervene or deliver me. He always met me in my pain. He never scolded me for pouring out my raw emotions but instead pulled me closer to His heart. In my cries of sorrow, He brought calm and comfort. He gave me supernatural peace and reminded me of all the times He had been faithful in the past.

In these moments of turmoil, my eyes were lifted as God spoke to my heart. Instead of seeing a problem too big to handle, He revealed a God far greater than the problem. My God can silence stormy seas with a word and breathe life into that which was dying. My God moves mountains and makes a way where there is no way. My God heals and restores. My God does the impossible and delights in the miraculous—and He is already working in your situation.

In the one true Almighty God, there is always victory. As you pray these *Rescue Prayers*, I hope you will find a safe space to lament and cry out to God, even as your heart is turned to know the rescue of His love and character. May your cries of sorrow be turned to praise as you declare God's goodness with great strength and certainty.

Each *Rescue Prayer* has been written in three parts: a lament or cry, a reminder of God's character, and a recognition or praise for what He will do in your situation. Modeled after the Psalms of King David, I hope that through the Holy Spirit, these prayers speak promise and peace into your situation. These thirty days of *Rescue Prayers* can be utilized daily or topically to address the precise challenge you are experiencing. The Lord will work in your circumstances!

May God forever be your anchor and rescue,

Christen

Christen M. Jeschke
Co-Creator, Rescue Prayers

P.S. I would love to hear how God heard and answered your prayers while working in your situation. Share your testimonies with us on social media @rescueprayers or visit us at www.rescueprayers.com.

PRAYER FOR
Facing a Difficult Diagnosis

"Be gracious to me, O Lord, for I am languishing;
O Lord, heal me, for my bones are shaking with terror.
My soul also is struck with terror, while you, O Lord—
how long? Turn, O Lord, save my life; deliver me
for the sake of your steadfast love."

PSALM 6:2-4 (NRSV)

"But let all who take refuge in you rejoice;
let them ever sing for joy. Spread your protection over them,
so that those who love your name may exult in you. For you
bless the righteous, O Lord; you cover them
with favor as with a shield."

PSALM 5:11-12 (NRSV)

Dear God,

I've just received an unexpected medical diagnosis, and I'm completely overwhelmed. My heart is pounding with fear, and it feels like my body is betraying me. I'm frozen with shock and disbelief. Why is this happening to me? It feels so unfair, and I'm terrified of what the future holds. The thought of what this means for my family and everyone I care about is unbearable. I don't know where to turn or how to process this. How do I even begin to talk about it with others? The heaviness of this news makes me feel both isolated and devastated. Lord, I'm desperately crying out for Your help! Please heal me—I need Your strength and comfort now more than ever.

Even in my fear and confusion, I hold onto the truth that You are a good God who delights in healing. I've heard of Your wondrous works and miracles, and I believe You can bring healing and restoration into my life as well. Please, give me the strength to face this challenge and the wisdom to make the right decisions. Guide me through the uncertainty and hold me close to Your heart. I feel lost but trust in Your loving plan, knowing that You can turn even the darkest moments into something beautiful.

Thank You for being with me during this incredibly difficult time. I need Your peace, which surpasses all understanding, to calm my racing thoughts and soothe my troubled heart. I place my trust in You, Lord, knowing that You will walk with me every step of the way.

In Jesus' name, I pray. Amen.

PRAYER FOR
Choosing the Right Treatment

"Answer me when I call, O God of my right!
You gave me room when I was in distress.
Be gracious to me, and hear my prayer."

PSALM 4:1 (NRSV)

"If any of you lacks wisdom, you should ask God,
who gives generously to all without finding fault,
and it will be given to you."

JAMES 1:5 (NIV)

Dear God,

Standing here, faced with all these treatment options for my diagnosis, I feel utterly overwhelmed. The choices are daunting, and I can't seem to find the right direction. My head is spinning with doubts and worries, and I'm terrified of making the wrong decision. What if I choose something that harms me? The fear of making a mistake is paralyzing. I desperately need Your wisdom and support to navigate this confusing and scary time. God, I need Your guidance now more than ever. Please walk me through every step of this journey, helping me see clearly and choose wisely.

In all this uncertainty, I find comfort in knowing that Your faithfulness and love never waver. You know what's best for me, and I trust that You will lead me down the right path. Please, give me clarity and calm my anxious heart. Surround me with the right people—wise doctors and advisors—who can help me make informed and sound decisions. I need Your peace to steady my heart and mind as I navigate these challenging choices.

Thank You, God, for always being with me, for Your endless strength, and Your unfailing love. You are the ultimate Healer, and I praise You for Your amazing healing power. I place my hope and confidence in You, trusting that You are in control and will guide me through whatever lies ahead.

In Jesus' name, I pray. Amen.

PRAYER FOR
Provision for Financial Burdens

"Therefore I tell you, do not worry about your life,
what you will eat or drink; or about your body,
what you will wear. Is not life more than food, and the body
more than clothes? Look at the birds of the air;
they do not sow or reap or store away in barns, and yet your
heavenly Father feeds them. Are you not much more valuable
than they? Can any one of you by worrying
add a single hour to your life?"

MATTHEW 6:25-27 (NIV)

"And my God will meet all your needs according to
the riches of his glory in Christ Jesus."

PHILIPPIANS 4:19 (NIV)

Dear God,

Today, I'm worried about by the sudden financial strain caused by my diagnosis. The looming medical bills, the cost of treatments, and other unexpected expenses are terrifying. I'm scared about how I'll manage everything, especially if I need to take time off work or if my health worsens. The uncertainty of what the future holds financially is crushing. The weight of not knowing how I'll keep up with these costs is unbearable. I feel trapped in a cycle of worry and fear. Lord, I desperately need Your wisdom and guidance to navigate these financial burdens. Please show me the way and provide the strength I need to get through this challenging time.

I hold onto Your promise that You will provide for my needs, and I'm grateful for that assurance. You've been faithful before, and I trust that You will continue to be with me now. Please help me lean on Your strength and make wise financial decisions. Surround me with supportive people and resources that can help lighten this heavy load. I feel so alone and scared, but I know that with Your help, I can find a way through this.

Thank You, God, for Your unfailing provision and the comfort of knowing You are with me. I praise You in advance for Your provision, and I trade my overwhelming worry for the peace that comes from Your enduring love and comforting reassurance.

In Jesus' name, I pray. Amen.

PRAYER FOR
Navigating Challenges at Work

"The Lord will guide you always; he will satisfy your needs in a sun-scorched land and will strengthen your frame. You will be like a well-watered garden, like a spring whose waters never fail."

ISAIAH 58:11 (NIV)

"But I know that the Lord has set apart the faithful for himself; the Lord hears when I call to him."

PSALM 4:3 (NRSV)

Dear God,

I'm grappling with the harsh reality of how my diagnosis is impacting my ability to work. It's terrifying because I don't want to lose my job, but these health challenges are making it increasingly difficult to keep up. The thought of losing the structure and routine my job provides is daunting, and the fear of losing income and the potential impact on my career down the road is weighing heavily on me. Feeling so limited by my health is frustrating, and the uncertainty of job disruption feels almost inevitable. I feel ashamed that I can't meet expectations like I used to, and it's hard not to let that shame consume me.

Lord, I know these feelings of shame and inadequacy don't come from You, but I need Your help now more than ever. Please grant me the wisdom to navigate this delicate balance between my health needs and work responsibilities. I trust in Your faithfulness and know You see and stand with me in these challenging times. You are my guide and support, and I believe You will lead me through this difficult season. I call on You, knowing You are present and active in my life. Help me make decisions that honor both my well-being and my professional obligations. Surround me with understanding and supportive coworkers and provide the resources I need to manage this burden.

As I cling to Your promises, I praise You for Your unwavering faithfulness and continuous work in every aspect of my life. My hope is in You, Lord, and I trust that You will see me through this.

In Jesus' name, I pray. Amen.

PRAYER FOR
Relief from Physical Pain

"My God, my God, why have you forsaken me?
Why are you so far from helping me, from the words
of my groaning? O my God, I cry by day, but you do not answer:
and by night but find no rest."

PSALM 22:1-2 (NRSV)

"The righteous cry out, and the Lord hears them;
he delivers them from all their troubles."

PSALM 34:17 (NIV)

Dear God,

I'm calling out to You because I desperately need You right now. The pain I'm in is overwhelming, consuming every thought and moment. It feels like there's no relief in sight, and it's wearing me down. This relentless pain isn't just physical; it's affecting my spirit, filling me with discouragement and robbing me of hope. I feel so alone in this struggle, crying out to You but feeling like my prayers aren't getting through. The days drag on, and the nights feel even longer as I battle this unyielding pain. I'm exhausted and worn out from this constant struggle, and I desperately need Your comfort and peace. Please, in Your mercy, hear my cries and ease my suffering.

Holy Spirit, I invite You into this moment of deep need. Even in the midst of this turmoil, I know that You are not far away. You are not distant or indifferent to what I'm going through. You understand every ache and groan in my body because You intimately created me. I thank You for being a God who heals and restores. As I wait for Your healing touch, give me the strength I need to endure. Help me shift my focus away from this pain and onto Your power and ability to bring relief.

My trust is in You, and I lean on Your promises. Even though it's hard, I hold onto the hope that You will bring me through this. I ask for Your presence to fill me with peace and comfort, reassuring me that I'm not alone in this journey. Empower me with Your strength, and renew my spirit with Your grace. Touch my body with Your healing power and restore me. Thank You, Lord, for Your unfailing love.

In Jesus' name, I pray. Amen.

PRAYER FOR
Improved Quality of Life

"Therefore let all who are faithful offer prayer to you; at a time of distress, the rush of mighty waters shall not reach them. You are a hiding place for me; you preserve me from trouble; you surround me with glad cries of deliverance."

PSALM 32:6-7 (NRSV)

"O Lord, you will hear the desire of the meek;
you will strengthen their heart,
you will incline your ear."

PSALM 10:17 (NRSV)

Dear God,

I am struggling. I long for a sense of normalcy and a return to the quality of life I had before my diagnosis. I don't feel like *me* anymore. I'm overwhelmed and depleted by the enormity of this burden. It's not just me who is affected; my family, loved ones, friends, and coworkers are feeling the impact of what I'm going through. They each handle it differently, and this often leads to a sense of isolation. My life has been turned upside down, and I feel disoriented by the rapid changes and upheaval that I can't control. There are days when I am so tired that I feel like I'm merely surviving. I don't know how much longer I can endure this without some relief.

Holy Spirit, when despair starts creeping in, remind me of Your promise that nothing can separate me from Your love. Fill me with Your peace that surpasses all understanding, and give me the courage to face each day with hope and strength. Your grace sustains me through it all. I need Your guidance and strength, for You are a mighty God who provides for all my needs. I know You hear my cries. Please help me find joy and purpose amid these challenges, knowing Your love and presence are always with me.

I surrender my fears, doubts, and uncertainties into Your loving hands. Renew my spirit, O Lord, and restore the joy of Your salvation in my life. Let Your presence fill me, bringing peace to my troubled heart. Thank You for being my refuge, strength, and ever-present help in trouble. I trust in Your love and power to bring healing and restoration to my life.

In Jesus' name, I pray. Amen.

PRAYER FOR
Fears About Death

"To you, Lord, I called; to the Lord I cried for mercy:
'What is gained if I am silenced, if I go down to the pit?
Will the dust praise you? Will it proclaim your faithfulness?
Hear, Lord, and be merciful to me;
Lord, be my help."

PSALM 30:8-10 (NIV)

"But I trusted in your steadfast love;
my heart rejoiced in your salvation. I will sing to the Lord,
because he has dealt bountifully with me."

PSALM 13:5-6 (NRSV)

Dear God,

Facing my mortality and the uncertainties it brings is incredibly difficult. The thought of leaving my loved ones behind breaks my heart and fills me with deep sorrow. I wrestle with these dark thoughts and feelings, sometimes finding myself consumed by worry and anxiety. I want to embrace Your presence and promises, but I also cherish the life You've given me and the moments I have with those I love. It's a struggle, Lord, and I'm crying out to You in the midst of all these fears and uncertainties. I feel lost and anxious, unsure how to find peace. Please, God, meet me in this place of fear and doubt.

Lord, please help me to trust in Your faithfulness and sovereignty. I know You are in control, even when everything feels out of my hands. Help me walk confidently, knowing that You have a plan for my good and that whatever happens, You will use all things for Your glory. Even as I cry out to You for rescue, teach me to live my life as a testament to Your grace and love. Let my life, even in its struggles, be a witness to Your power and goodness so that there may be an eternal impact on all those I encounter. Remove my fear, Lord, and replace it with a supernatural faith only You can provide. I long for Your peace to fill my heart and calm my anxieties about the future.

Holy Spirit, fill me with Your presence and comfort. Surround me with Your love and assurance, reminding me I am never alone. Help me to find peace in the knowledge that my life is in Your hands and that You have a purpose for every moment I am given. Give me the courage to testify boldly of Your goodness and to live each day fully.

In Jesus' name, I pray. Amen.

PRAYER FOR
Emotional Well-Being

"Why, my soul, are you downcast?
Why so disturbed within me? Put your hope in God,
for I will yet praise him, my Savior and my God.

PSALM 43:5 (NIV)

"You show me the path of life. In your presence
there is fullness of joy; in your right hand
are pleasures forevermore."

PSALM 16:11 (NRSV)

Dear God,

I need You! I am discouraged by my health situation, and my stomach is in knots with inner turmoil. These health challenges are taking a heavy toll on my emotional well-being, leaving me anxious and feeling down. The uncertainty ahead makes me feel overwhelmed and exhausted. I'm caught up in worry and can't seem to shake off this anxiety that grips me day and night. I feel trapped in a cycle of fear and doubt, and it's draining my spirit. Lord, I desperately long for Your supernatural peace and comfort in this time of distress.

I cry out to You, Lord, for relief from these overwhelming thoughts. Help me to fix my focus on You and Your mighty power, knowing that You are greater than any challenge I face. I trust You to carry my burdens and replace my worries with joy and praise. Speak words of love and kindness over me, reminding me that You are here, fighting for me and guiding me through each step of this diagnosis. Infuse me with Your courage and strength to face each day, knowing that You deliver me from anxiety, depression, and fear.

I bring these struggles to You in prayer, seeking Your presence and finding comfort in Your goodness. You turn my sorrows into joy and my fears into rejoicing. I surrender to You, Lord, and rest in Your unfailing love. Thank You for being my refuge and strength, my ever-present help in trouble.

In Jesus' name, I pray. Amen.

Day 9

PRAYER FOR

My Family and Relationships

"Relent, Lord! How long will it be? Have compassion on your servants. Satisfy us in the morning with your unfailing love, that we may sing for joy and be glad all our days. Make us glad for as many days as you have afflicted us, for as many years as we have seen trouble. May your deeds be shown to your servants, your splendor to their children."

PSALM 90:13-16 (NIV)

"Posterity will serve him; future generations will be told about the Lord. They will proclaim his righteousness, declaring to a people yet unborn: He has done it!

PSALM 22:30-31 (NIV)

Dear God,

I come before You today, praying for my family and relationships. The weight of my diagnosis has created strain and exhaustion, not just for me but for everyone I hold dear. The tension and worry hang over us, making it hard to find peace. We all feel the burden of this situation, and it's affecting our connections with each other. We desperately need Your presence and strength to renew our spirits and bring us closer together. Please minister to each of us individually, touching our hearts and minds with Your healing power, and draw us together as a unified family. Help us to navigate this challenging journey with grace, compassion, and unity, supporting one another through all the ups and downs.

Grant us the wisdom to communicate openly and honestly, listen with empathy, and extend forgiveness and grace when needed. You are a God of gracious love, and I pray that we can reflect that love and grace to each other, uplifting one another as You uplift us. Let our home be filled with

Your peace and Your presence, healing any brokenness and mending any divisions. I praise You for being a God who heals and restores, and I trust that You will bring reconciliation where there is hurt and unity where there is discord.

Thank You, Lord, for the precious gift of family and relationships. Help me cherish every moment and prioritize our time together, knowing how fleeting life can be. May Your presence dwell among us, bringing joy, unity, and strength to our hearts and home. Guide us in love, deepen our faith, and help us to lean on You and each other as we navigate these uncertain times.

In Jesus' name, I pray. Amen.

PRAYER FOR
Those Caring for Me

"He gives strength to the weary and increases the power of the weak. Even youths grow tired and weary, and young men stumble and fall; but those who hope in the Lord will renew their strength. They will soar on wings like eagles; they will run and not grow weary, they will walk and not be faint."

ISAIAH 40:29-31 (NIV)

"The Lord is my strength and my shield;
my heart trusts in him, and he helps me. My heart leaps for joy,
and with my song I praise him."

PSALM 28:7 (NIV)

Dear God,

My heart is filled with gratitude and concern for the loving people who have stepped up to help me during my illness. I see the exhaustion in their eyes as they tirelessly support me. Their efforts to comfort and uplift are so evident, yet I can't help but notice the weariness they carry. It's heartbreaking to see them give so much, even as they navigate their own emotions and challenges. The guilt of feeling like a burden weighs on me, and I desperately need Your courage and strength to lean on their support, trusting that You will also renew their spirits.

Lord, I am deeply thankful for these support systems You've placed in my life—they are tangible reminders of Your constant care and provision. Please bless these dear helpers with Your supernatural strength and endurance as they care for me. I know they give from a place of love, but I see the toll it takes on them. Pour out Your Spirit upon them, refreshing their weary souls and empowering them for every task they undertake on my behalf. Help them feel Your presence and know that their efforts are not in vain and are deeply appreciated and seen.

Fill us all with courage and perseverance, especially on days when the burden feels too heavy to bear. You are our strength and our ever-present help in times of trouble. I trust in Your promise to restore and revitalize us, for You are a mighty God, capable of renewing our strength and uplifting our spirits. May Your love and grace surround us, giving us the resilience we need to face each day.

In Jesus' name, I pray. Amen.

PRAYER FOR
Strength Navigating Loss of Independence

"Be merciful to me, Lord, for I am in distress;
my eyes grow weak with sorrow, my soul and body with grief.
My life is consumed by anguish and my years by groaning; my strength fails because of my affliction,
and my bones grow weak.

PSALM 31:9-10 (NIV)

"But blessed is the one who trusts in the Lord,
whose confidence is in him. They will be like a tree planted
by the water that sends out its roots by the stream. It does
not fear when heat comes; its leaves are always green.
It has no worries in a year of drought and
never fails to bear fruit."

JEREMIAH 17:7-8 (NIV)

Dear God,

I'm coming to You, grappling with the loss of my independence due to this diagnosis. It's incredibly difficult to depend on others for even the simplest tasks. I feel so frustrated and vulnerable, trying to navigate this new reality where I can't do things independently like I used to. The fear of becoming a burden to those I love weighs heavily on me, and it's hard to shake the uncertainty about how I'll manage in the future. The loss of control over my own life fills me with anxiety and sadness, and I find myself questioning how I will cope with these changes. Please, God, give me the strength and courage to face each day with grace and resilience, even when the path ahead seems daunting.

Amid these challenges, I cling to Your promise that You are my strength forever. Even in my weakness, You lift me with Your unfailing love. Help me let go of my pride and self-reliance and embrace the strength that comes from trusting in You. Remind me that true independence doesn't mean doing everything on my own but instead relying on Your strength and leaning on Your everlasting arms. This transition is hard, and I need Your help to adjust and find peace in this new way of living.

Thank You, Lord, for the loved ones who support me and walk alongside me with their care and assistance. Their presence is a blessing, and I am grateful for the love and compassion they show. May Your presence be with me always, guiding me through this season of dependence and teaching me valuable lessons about humility and trust. Help me see this time as an opportunity to grow closer to You and those around me.

In Jesus' name, I pray. Amen.

PRAYER FOR
Finding the Right Care

"For he did not despise or abhor the affliction
of the afflicted; he did not hide his face from me,
but heard when I cried to him."

PSALM 22:24 (NRSV)

"I will instruct you and teach you in the way
you should go; I will counsel you with
my loving eye on you."

PSALM 32:8 (NIV)

Dear God,

I come before You, burdened with deep concerns about accessing the care I desperately need. The path ahead feels uncertain, and I am worried about finding the right specialists, the quality of treatment facilities, and whether the resources available will be sufficient. The complexities of navigating the healthcare system are overwhelming, and the anxiety of not receiving timely and effective care is stressful. I worry about what lies ahead and the potential challenges and setbacks I may face. The anxiety is relentless, making it hard to find peace. Lord, I give You my fear, knowing it does nothing but drag me down and cloud my judgment.

I ask for Your guidance and intervention in every step of this journey. Your Word assures me that You will supply every need according to Your riches in glory. I hold onto this promise, trusting in Your provision and wisdom to guide me through this challenging time. Please give me clarity of mind to make the right decisions regarding my healthcare and peace in my heart as I navigate the system. Help me find the right doctors, treatments, and resources that align with Your will for my life. I know You are my strength, courage, and steadfast rock in these uncertain times.

Jesus, You are my advocate and protector, and I praise You for being with me through every appointment, procedure, and waiting period. Your presence is a constant reassurance that I am not alone in this journey. May Your healing power be evident in Your life and according to Your perfect timing. Guide me with Your wisdom, and grant me the patience and faith to trust in Your plan.

In Jesus' name, I pray. Amen.

PRAYER FOR
Wisdom in Medical Decisions

"Make me to know your ways, O Lord; teach me your paths.
Lead me in your truth, and teach me, for you are the God of my
salvation; for you I wait all day long."

PSALM 25:4-5 (NRSV)

"Whether you turn to the right or to the left,
your ears will hear a voice behind you, saying,
'This is the way; walk in it.'"

ISAIAH 30:21 (NIV)

Dear God,

I come to You feeling burdened by the daunting task of making crucial healthcare decisions. The path before me is filled with uncertainty, and I am deeply troubled by the weight of the choices I must make—decisions that could profoundly impact my health and future. I feel lost, not knowing which way to turn or the best course of action. My mind is a whirlwind of questions: How do I choose the right treatments? Will they work? What if I make the wrong choice, and it worsens my situation? I feel so alone in this journey. Please, Lord, I need Your divine clarity and guidance to navigate these complex and confusing medical choices.

You are the God of wisdom and understanding, and I know that You are intimately aware of my situation and the concerns that plague my heart. Help me to surrender my understanding and fears, trusting fully in You. I trust You, Lord, believing You will guide me to the right healthcare professionals and treatments that align with Your perfect will for my life.

You are my Healer and Sustainer, who holds my future in Your hands. Strengthen my faith, O Lord, and grant me the peace that surpasses all understanding as I navigate this challenging season.

May Your wisdom shine brightly through every decision I make, illuminating the path You have set before me. Let Your power be evident in my life, guiding me with grace and assurance. I pray that through this journey, Your name will be glorified and Your purpose fulfilled in my life. Thank You for being my steadfast rock and source of hope.

In Jesus' name, I pray. Amen.

PRAYER FOR

Accepting Changes to Future Plans

"Commit your work to the Lord,
and your plans will be established."

PROVERBS 16:3 (ESV)

"I believe that I shall see the goodness of the Lord in the land of the living. Wait for the Lord; be strong, and let your heart take courage; wait for the Lord!"

PSALM 27:13-14 (NRSV)

Dear God,

I come before You with deep concerns about how my current medical situation will impact my future plans. The dreams and aspirations I once held dear are now clouded with uncertainty. It's difficult to face the reality that my life may never be the same, and the future I envisioned seems so distant now. I feel lost and confused, unsure whether to continue planning and hoping for my career goals, travel dreams, and personal milestones or to simply take each day as it comes. These unknowns press uneasily on my heart, and I desperately need Your guidance and clarity. Lord, help me navigate this season of uncertainty and align my future with Your perfect will. Show me the path You have set for me, and help me trust that Your plans are far greater than mine.

    I praise You, Lord because You are the Alpha and Omega, the one who knows my beginning and end. You see the whole picture of my life, and You promise to walk with me through every high and low. Your

Word assures me that You work all things together for good for those who love You and are called according to Your purpose. Even when the path ahead feels overwhelming, I find peace knowing that You are in control, orchestrating every detail for my good and Your glory. Strengthen my faith and remind me daily that Your plans are good, filled with hope and a future.

Holy Spirit, fill me with Your wisdom and supernatural peace as I make decisions about my future. Give me the courage to let go of my own plans and embrace the beautiful journey You have laid out for me. May Your presence be a constant reminder that I am never alone and that You are always guiding me toward Your purpose.

In Jesus' name, I pray. Amen.

PRAYER FOR

My Changing Physical Appearance

"O Lord, all my longing is known to you; my sighing is not hidden from you. My heart throbs, my strength fails me; as for the light of my eyes—it also has gone from me."

PSALM 38:9-10 (NRSV)

"The Lord does not look at the things people look at. People look at the outward appearance,
but the Lord looks at the heart."

1 SAMUEL 16:7B (NIV)

Dear God,

I am concerned about my physical appearance, which has been significantly affected by my health challenges. The changes in my body have shaken my confidence and caused me to feel insecure and distressed. Every day, I struggle with the way I look, fearing how others perceive me and worrying about the impact on my self-worth and relationships. It's hard to face the mirror and accept the person staring back. I feel like I'm losing a part of myself. Help me find peace and acceptance by seeing myself through Your eyes–the vision of a loving creator.

You are the God who looks beyond the surface, who knows and loves us in our entirety. Your Word tells me I am fearfully and wonderfully made, created in Your image. Help me to find my value in being Your beloved child. In a world that often values outward appearance, please remind me that true attractiveness comes from within—from a heart filled with kindness, love, and compassion. Teach me to focus on cultivating these qualities rather than being consumed by physical concerns.

Holy Spirit, I invite You into my heart to renew my sense of self-worth and confidence. Fill me with a deep understanding of my identity in Christ, and help me to rest in the knowledge that I am deeply loved and cherished by You. Let Your love be the foundation upon which I build my confidence and self-esteem. May Your presence in my life radiate through every interaction, reflecting the inner beauty You've placed within me. Thank You, Lord, for loving me just as I am and reminding me that my true worth is found in You alone.

In Jesus' name, I pray. Amen.

PRAYER FOR
Establishing Healthy Coping Methods

"Cast your burden on the Lord, and he will sustain you; he will never permit the righteous to be moved."

PSALM 55:22 (ESV)

"I waited patiently for the Lord; he inclined to me and heard my cry. He drew me up from the desolate pit, out of the miry bog, and set my feet upon a rock, making my steps secure."

PSALM 40:1-2 (NSRV)

Dear God,

I need help coping with this diagnosis. I've been searching desperately for ways to manage, but nothing seems to ease the strain for long. I'm tired, stressed, worn out, and discouraged. It's not just the physical pain that wears me down—it's the emotional toll that drains my spirit and tests my endurance. I miss the normalcy of my old routine and the stability that seems so distant now. Every day feels like a battle just to keep going. Lord, I need Your help to find healthy ways to cope during this difficult season. Please, bring me relief and peace.

Lord, You see every struggle, every anxious thought that races through my mind. I'm asking for Your wisdom, Lord, to help me see clearly how to proceed. Show me the path to take and guide my days. I need Your discipline to choose healthy ways to cope with this overwhelming strain. Grant me the strength to face each moment with courage and resilience, even when it feels like too much to bear. Help me find solace in Your presence and comfort in Your promises. I know Your grace is sufficient for me, and I cling to that hope even when everything else feels uncertain.

Holy Spirit, I invite You into this space of turmoil and confusion. Fill me with Your peace that surpasses all understanding. Help me to rest in Your promises and to trust in Your unfailing care and strength. Remind me that I am not alone in this journey and that You are always with me, providing comfort and support. Guide me to resources, people, and practices that will help me manage this stress in a way that honors You. Thank You for being my ever-present help in times of need. I place my burdens and worries in Your capable hands, trusting that You will see me through.

In Jesus' name, I pray. Amen.

PRAYER FOR
Guidance Managing My Medications

"But he said to me, 'My grace is sufficient for you,
for my power is made perfect in weakness.' Therefore
I will boast all the more gladly of my weaknesses,
so that the power of Christ may rest upon me."

2 CORINTHIANS 12:9 (ESV)

"Teach me your way, O Lord, that I may walk in your truth; give
me an undivided heart to revere your name. I give thanks to you,
O Lord my God, with my whole heart,
and I will glorify your name forever."

PSALM 86:11-12 (NRSV)

Dear God,

I need help processing anxiety about managing my medications. The treatment plan I'm following feels confusing and complicated, and I'm so worried about keeping up with it correctly. The fear of potential side effects and interactions is stressful. I find myself constantly anxious about forgetting doses or making a mistake that could negatively impact my health. Lord, I need Your guidance and strength to navigate this challenging healing journey. Please help me to manage my medication and dosages with clarity and confidence.

You are the God who gives grace to the weak and shows Your strength in our vulnerability. I ask for Your grace to help me stay diligent and disciplined in adhering to my treatment plan. Give me the clarity of mind to keep track of my medications and the courage to trust in Your wisdom and provision. Help me to find peace in knowing that You are in control, even when I feel overwhelmed. May Your peace fill my heart and guard me against fears and anxieties. Remind me that You are holding me in Your hands and that You are the ultimate healer.

Please guide me each day. Fill me with Your presence. Empower me to release my worries into Your care and trust Your constant presence and support. Thank You, Lord, for Your sustaining grace that upholds me and for the assurance that You are always watching over my health. Strengthen my faith, and help me to rest in Your love and provision.

In Jesus' name, I pray. Amen.

Day 18

PRAYER FOR

Protection for My Children

"Let me abide in your tent forever, find refuge under
the shelter of your wings. For you, O God, have heard my vows;
you have given me the heritage of those
who fear your name."

PSALM 61:4-5 (NRSV)

"All your children will be taught by the Lord,
and great will be their peace."

ISAIAH 54:13 (NIV)

Dear God,

I'm coming to You with a deep concern for my children and the challenges we're all facing. Lord, You know their vulnerability and the tender state of their hearts. The uncertainty of our situation is unimaginably complex, and I can see its impact on their emotions and spirit. I'm worried about how all this instability is affecting them, not just emotionally and spiritually, but in their everyday lives. The fear and confusion are palpable, and it's heartbreaking to witness. Please, Lord, protect their hearts and minds from worry. Surround them with Your love and peace, and give them the strength and resilience they need to overcome this tough time. Draw near to them, and let them feel Your undeniable presence, comforting them in ways only You can.

You are a loving creator who cares deeply for Your children. I trust in Your promise to be our refuge and strength, and I know that You hold my children in Your protective embrace. Help me to support them, providing the reassurance and love they need during this challenging period. Show me how to reflect Your heart and grace in every word and action so they can see Your love through me. Give me the wisdom to guide them with patience and compassion, nurturing their faith and helping them grow stronger in You.

Holy Spirit, please fill our home with Your peace and presence. Comfort my children in moments of fear and doubt, and strengthen their faith in Your unfailing love. Thank You, Father, for being a good and loving provider, always watching over my children and me. I trust that You will continue to protect and guide us through these uncertain times, keeping us close to Your heart.

In Jesus' name, I pray. Amen.

PRAYER FOR
Spiritual Strength Amid Doubt

"How long, Lord? Will you forget me forever?
How long will you hide your face from me?
How long must I wrestle with my thoughts and
day after day have sorrow in my heart?"

PSALM 13:1-2A (NIV)

"Am I a God at hand, declares the Lord,
and not a God far away? Can a man hide himself in
secret places so that I cannot see him? declares the Lord.
Do I not fill heaven and earth? declares the Lord."

JEREMIAH 23:23-24 (ESV)

Dear God,

I'm pouring out my heart to You today, feeling overwhelmed with spiritual concerns and doubts. It seems like You're far away, and I'm struggling to feel the peace of Your presence. My heart is heavy, and bitterness is creeping in as I wrestle with the situation I'm in. I confess this to You and ask for Your forgiveness, Lord. Please draw near to me and powerfully reveal Your presence. Help me not feel alone but know that I am seen by You and comforted by Your love. Amid this sadness, help me remember Your faithfulness and trust that You are near, even when it feels like You're distant.

For I know that You are close to those who are hurting, and You rescue those who feel crushed in spirit. Lord, help me to trust in Your unfailing love and find comfort in Your presence. Renew my spirit, O God, and remind me of Your promises. Guide me through this season of doubt and strengthen me to walk confidently in Your truth. I long for Your peace and assurance, and I know that only You can provide the comfort I seek. Surround me with Your presence, Lord, and help me rest, knowing that You are always with me, even in my darkest moments.

Holy Spirit, please fill me with Your peace and calm my anxious heart. Help me to surrender my fears and doubts to You, trusting that You are in control. Pour out Your Spirit on me, Lord, and hold me close to Your heart. I praise You for being a God who sees me and draws near. Thank You for Your never-ending love and compassion. Be with me in my distress, and hold me tight in Your loving embrace.

In Jesus' name, I pray. Amen.

PRAYER FOR
Calm in Loss of Control

"Save me, O God, for the waters have come up to my neck. I sink in the miry depths, where there is no foothold. I have come into the deep waters; the floods engulf me."

PSALM 69:1-2 (NIV)

"He reached down from on high, he took me; he drew me out of mighty waters...He brought me out into a broad place; he delivered me because he delighted in me."

PSALM 18:16 & 19 (NRSV)

Dear God,

My circumstances are overwhelming, and I can't see a way out. Fear and uncertainty have taken hold, and it's like I'm losing my grip on reality. The ground feels shaky beneath me, and I can't seem to find solid footing. It's so hard to let go and surrender this situation to You, Lord. I want to trust that You are in control, even when everything around me feels chaotic and uncertain. I need Your help to release this burden and place my circumstances in Your capable hands, knowing there's no safer place to be.

You are the God who holds everything together. Please give me the strength to stop trying to manage everything on my own. I know my attempts to control are futile and only add to my stress and anxiety. Teach me to surrender to Your will and timing, trusting that Your plans are perfect and far beyond my understanding. Help me to rest in the knowledge that You are my refuge and strength, an ever-present help in times of trouble.

Holy Spirit, fill me with Your peace and calm my anxious thoughts. Help me to trust entirely in God's sovereignty and goodness. Guide my heart to a place of surrender, where I can let go of my fears and rest in the assurance that God is in control. Thank You, Lord, for being my anchor, shelter in the storm, and constant guide. Fill my heart and mind with Your peace as I learn to fully trust You each day.

In Jesus' name, I pray. Amen.

Day 21

PRAYER FOR
Comfort in Isolation and Loneliness

"Where can I go from your Spirit? Where can I flee from your
presence? If I go up to the heavens, you are there;
if I make my bed in the depths, you are there. If I rise
on the wings of the dawn, if I settle on the far side
of the sea, even there your hand will guide me,
your right hand will hold me fast."

PSALM 139:7-10 (NIV)

"It is the Lord who goes before you.
He will be with you;
he will not leave you or forsake you.
Do not fear or be dismayed."

DEUTERONOMY 31:8 (ESV)

Dear God,

I feel isolated and alone. Being apart from loved ones and feeling disconnected from my community is tough. The loneliness can be overwhelming, and sometimes it feels like no one understands what I am going through. In these moments, I cling to Your promise that You are always with me. You shield me from trouble and surround me with songs of deliverance. Lord, I desperately need to deeply sense Your presence during this season of solitude. Remind me that even when I'm physically alone, You are near and watching over me, providing comfort and strength.

Despite this isolation, I praise You because You are an ever-present God who is attentive to my needs. You promise never to abandon me, and I hold onto that assurance. Please fill my heart with the certainty that I am not alone, for You are by my side always. Help me experience Your presence in a powerful and tangible way, especially when the loneliness overwhelms me. Give me the wisdom to find creative ways to connect with others, even from a distance, and to be a source of encouragement and love to those around me.

Holy Spirit, wrap me in Your peace and strengthen me with Your joy as I navigate these challenging times. Help me rest in knowing that You are my safe haven and the source of my hope. Thank You, Lord, for being my constant companion and refuge. I trust in Your unfailing love and the promise that You will never leave or forsake me.

In Jesus' name, I pray. Amen.

Day 22

PRAYER FOR
Release from Guilt and Shame

"For I know my transgressions, and my sin is ever before me. Against you, you only, have I sinned and done what is evil in your sight, so that you may be justified in your words and blameless in your judgment."

PSALM 51:3-4 (ESV)

"Therefore, there is now no condemnation for those who are in Christ Jesus, because through Christ Jesus the law of the Spirit who gives life has set you free from the law of sin and death."

ROMANS 8:1-2 (NIV)

Dear God,

I come to You wrestling with guilt and shame. My mind is filled with thoughts of mistakes and shortcomings, especially as I reflect on my life and mortality. I wonder if I could have made different choices or done things better—this burden of wrongs nags at me, and I long to make amends. I confess these feelings to You and ask for Your forgiveness and cleansing. I need Your help to release this weight of guilt and fully embrace Your grace and mercy. Please give me the courage to seek forgiveness from those I've hurt and to work toward healing and restoration. Show me where I need to confess and repent, guiding me to walk in freedom from shame.

You are a God of compassion and forgiveness and are always ready to forgive when we turn to You. I am deeply grateful that Your mercies are new every morning and that You offer conviction rather than condemnation. Please strengthen me to forgive myself and let go of the shame that binds me. Remind me that I am made new in Christ, washed clean by His sacrifice. Help me to accept Your forgiveness fully and to see myself through Your eyes, free from the burdens of past mistakes.

Holy Spirit, fill me with the assurance of Your love and the freedom that comes from Your forgiveness. Help me to live each day in the light of Your grace, embracing the new life You offer. Thank You, Lord, for Your unconditional love that covers my faults and failures. Guide me to live in the freedom of Your forgiveness and grace, and help me to extend that same grace to others.

In Jesus' name, I pray. Amen.

PRAYER FOR
Rest on Sleepless Nights

"When I was in distress, I sought the Lord;
at night I stretched out untiring hands,
and I would not be comforted."

PSALM 77:2 (NIV)

"You will keep in perfect peace those whose minds
are steadfast, because they trust in you."

ISAIAH 26:3 (NIV)

Dear God,

In the stillness of the night, when sleep escapes me, I struggle with more than just worries. The pain and discomfort from illness, combined with anxiety, make restful sleep seem impossible. My body aches, and my mind races, filled with fears and concerns. The quiet darkness amplifies everything, making the hours unbearably long. I come to You, seeking comfort and peace, longing for the rest that my weary body and troubled mind desperately need. The pain seems relentless, and the anxiety keeps my mind on edge, making it hard to let go and relax. I feel completely depleted, and I need Your help more than ever.

Yet, even on these challenging nights, I hold onto the truth that You are with me. Help me to trust in Your presence and find refuge in Your unfailing love. Let Your peace wash over me, quieting my racing thoughts and easing my physical discomfort. I surrender all my fears, pain, and worries into Your capable hands, knowing that You care for me deeply.

Instead of wrestling with what I cannot control, I release everything to You, trusting in Your wisdom and strength. Quiet my mind and soothe my body, Lord. Turn my thoughts towards Your faithfulness and love, reminding me that You are my healer and comforter. Protect my heart and mind through the night so I may find moments of rest and wake up with renewed strength and hope.

Holy Spirit, I invite Your comforting presence to envelop me, bringing tranquility to my soul and relief to my body. Guide me into a peaceful sleep, free from the burdens of pain and anxiety. May Your presence be a balm to my aching body and calm my anxious thoughts.

In Jesus' name, I pray. Amen.

Day 24

PRAYER FOR
Mental Clarity and Focus

"And the peace of God, which transcends all understanding, will guard your hearts and your minds in Christ Jesus."

PHILIPPIANS 4:7 (NIV)

"Listen, my son, accept what I say, and the years of your life will be many. I instruct you in the way of wisdom and lead you along straight paths. When you walk, your steps will not be hampered; when you run, you will not stumble."

PROVERBS 4:10-12 (NIV)

Dear God,

I desperately seek Your wisdom and clarity for my cognitive function. My thoughts often feel scattered and foggy, leaving me needing help to focus and think clearly. It's unsettling and frustrating not to have control over my own mind, especially when I need to make important decisions or simply get through the day. The constant mental fog weighs heavily on me, making it hard to engage fully with life. Please, Lord, lift this cloudiness from me and replace it with Your sober thought and understanding. I bring You my concerns about my cognitive function, asking for Your guidance and support. Help me to manage my thoughts and mental processes in a way that honors You and reflects Your truth.

I praise You because You are a God of order and peace. You transform confusion into clear wisdom and bring light to the darkest corners of my mind. When challenges and overwhelming situations arise, I turn to You, seeking Your calming presence. I don't want anxiety and worry to dominate my thoughts or distract me from Your truth. Help me to fix my gaze firmly on You, standing strong in the knowledge that You bring peace and clarity to my mind.

Holy Spirit, I invite You to renew my mind daily. Guide me to align my thoughts with Your will, and let Your Word be the foundation of my mental health. When my thoughts become chaotic, be my calm. Fill me with Your peace that surpasses all understanding, and help me to trust that You are in control. Thank You for being my source of wisdom and strength and for Your unwavering love and care.

In Jesus' name, I pray. Amen.

PRAYER FOR

Restoration of Relational Intimacy

"Be completely humble and gentle; be patient,
bearing with one another in love. Make every effort to keep the
unity of the Spirit through the bond of peace."

EPHESIANS 4:2-3 (NIV)

"And over all these virtues put on love,
which binds them all together in perfect unity."

COLOSSIANS 3:14 (NIV)

Dear God,

I come to You burdened with the challenges I'm facing in physical intimacy due to this medical diagnosis. The illness has placed a strain on both my physical and emotional connections, leaving me feeling distant and disheartened. It's heartbreaking to feel this gap growing in my relationship, making me feel isolated and alone. The lack of intimacy makes me question my worth and desirability. Lord, I need Your wisdom and grace to navigate these complexities. Please heal any hurt or insecurities that arise and help communication be open and bonds be strengthened amid these challenges. I feel so lost and in need of Your guidance.

Lord, I know that intimacy is a precious gift from You, a beautiful reflection of Your love and unity. Guide me to cherish and nurture this aspect of my relationship, even when the physical side is hindered. You designed intimacy in marriage to be a source of joy and connection, and I long to experience that fully. Help me to see beyond the physical limitations and to focus on the deeper emotional and spiritual connection. Pour out Your love, comfort, and strength into our relationship, fostering closeness even when physical intimacy may be limited. Your love is selfless and pure; help me to embody that same selflessness and patience in this area.

Holy Spirit, I ask for Your presence and power to work through relationships. Let Your love bridge any gaps and heal any wounds. Teach me to honor You in every aspect of my life, including my relationship. May intimacy be grounded in Your truth and love, reflecting the beauty of Your design. Give me the courage to face these challenges in unity, leaning on Your strength and wisdom.

In Jesus' name, I pray. Amen.

PRAYER FOR
Provision of Reliable Transportation

"Then they cried to the Lord in their trouble,
and he delivered them from their distress."

PSALM 107:6 (ESV)

"For God alone my soul waits in silence,
for my hope is from him. He alone is my rock
and my salvation, my fortress; I shall not be shaken.
On God rests my deliverance and my honor;
my mighty rock, my refuge is in God."

PSALM 62:5-8 (NRSV)

Dear God,

I need help getting from place to place. Transportation challenges have become a significant obstacle, disrupting my daily routines and responsibilities. It's not just about the inconvenience—it's about the stress and anxiety that come with unreliable vehicles, financial limitations, and the seemingly endless stream of appointments and logistical issues. Every day feels like an uphill battle, and it is frustrating. I need Your help!

Lord, I know You're always there for me, providing and sustaining me through every situation. I'm so grateful for Your unwavering presence in my life, especially during these difficult times. Even when things seem impossible, I trust You'll find a way. Your Word reassures me of Your faithfulness and deep care for every aspect of my life. So, I'm putting my transportation needs in Your hands, trusting You to guide and provide for me. Please step in and lead me to practical solutions. Open doors for the help and resources I need, whether it's reliable transportation, financial assistance, or a support system to ease the burden—please provide. I lean on Your wisdom and timing, knowing You're working for my good, even when I can't see the way ahead.

Holy Spirit, fill me with Your supernatural peace and comfort. Remind me that I'm not alone in this struggle and that You are right beside me every step of the way. Give me the strength to face each day with hope and determination, trusting in Your love and provision. Thank You for Your constant love and for being my rock when I need You the most.

In Jesus' name, I pray. Amen.

PRAYER FOR
Help with Nutritional Changes

"He provides food for those who fear him;
he remembers his covenant forever.
He has shown his people the power of his works,
in giving them the inheritance of the nations.
The works of his hands are faithful and just;
all his precepts are trustworthy."

PSALM 111:5-7 (ESV)

"For he satisfies the thirsty and fills
the hungry with good things."

PSALM 107:9 (NIV)

Dear God,

I come to You struggling with the dietary challenges that have come with my unexpected medical diagnosis. This illness has thrown my routines off completely, leaving me unsure about how to nourish my body properly to support healing and overall health. The changes I need to make are daunting. I worry about finding the right foods that will provide the strength and vitality I need while also fitting within my treatment plan. Lord, I need Your wisdom and guidance to navigate these new dietary restrictions and requirements. Help me find the energy and determination to explore and adhere to the best options for my condition.

Thank You for being a loving God who cares deeply about every detail of my life, including my physical well-being. Your Word reminds me that You provide for all my needs, and I hold onto that promise as I seek to maintain my health through this journey. Please nourish my body and soul with the right foods and spiritual sustenance. Lord, I praise You for Your faithfulness, and I trust that You will walk with me through this challenging time, offering Your support and strength.

Holy Spirit, guide me in making dietary choices that honor both my body and faith in Your loving care. Help me embrace this journey with a sense of peace, knowing that You are with me. May my efforts to nourish myself reflect my trust in Your provision and bring glory to Your name. Thank You for being my constant source of strength and comfort.

In Jesus' name, I pray. Amen.

Day 28

PRAYER FOR
Guidance for Alternative Therapies

"Let the morning bring me word of your unfailing love,
for I have put my trust in you. Show me the way
I should go, for to you I entrust my life."

PSALM 143:8 (NIV)

"I am your servant; give me understanding,
so that I may know your decrees."

PSALM 119:125 (NRSV)

Dear God,

As I continue to navigate these unexpected health challenges, I find myself exploring various alternative therapies and treatments. The array of options—natural remedies, holistic practices, and innovative therapies—are difficult to sort through. I am unsure of what direction to go in. I need Your wisdom and guidance to discern which approaches align with Your will for my healing. The uncertainty and fear of making the wrong choice weigh heavily on me. I worry about the safety and effectiveness of these treatments and whether they will truly aid in my recovery. Please give me clarity and peace of mind as I assess each option. Lead me to practitioners who work with integrity and compassion and can offer the best care and guidance.

Thank You, Lord, for being the Great Physician, the ultimate healer who cares deeply about every aspect of my health. Your Word reassures me that You are with me in every situation, and I trust in Your provision and guidance as I venture into these alternative paths of healing. Please close doors to any treatments that could be harmful or ineffective and open doors to those that will truly benefit me. Help me trust in Your perfect plan for my health, even when the future is uncertain. I lean on Your wisdom and direction, knowing You hold my life in Your hands.

Holy Spirit, I ask for Your comforting presence and guidance. Infuse me with Your peace as I make these decisions. May Your healing power flow through every treatment I choose, bringing restoration and wholeness to my body and soul. I surrender my fears and anxieties to You, trusting You will lead me to the right paths. Thank You for Your unwavering love.

In Jesus' name, I pray. Amen.

Day 29

PRAYER FOR
Faith Amid Doubt and Uncertainty

"God is our refuge and strength, an ever-present help in trouble. Therefore we will not fear, though the earth give way and the mountains fall into the heart of the sea, though its waters roar and foam and the mountains quake with their surging."

PSALM 46:1-3 (NIV)

"Therefore we do not lose heart. Though outwardly we are wasting away, yet inwardly we are being renewed day by day. For our light and momentary troubles are achieving for us an eternal glory that far outweighs them all. So we fix our eyes not on what is seen, but on what is unseen, since what is seen is temporary, but what is unseen is eternal."

2 CORINTHIANS 4:16-18 (NIV)

Dear God,

I am uncertain about what the future holds. The future seems shrouded in questions, and it's hard not to worry about what each new day might bring—more challenges, difficult treatments, or unexpected news that could alter my life even further. This uncertainty fills me with anxiety and dread, making it difficult to find peace or focus on the present. Lord, I feel lost and unsure how to navigate these turbulent waters. The unknowns weigh heavily on my spirit, and I constantly wonder how I will manage it all. I need You to remove these moments of doubt and fear.

But despite these fears, I choose to lay them at Your feet, knowing that You hold my future in Your hands. Help me release my grip on these uncertainties and trust that You control every part of my life, even when things seem unclear. Your Word reminds me that You are my Rock, Fortress, Strength, and Protector. I find a constant and enduring love that never wavers in You, even when everything around me does. Lord, give me the courage to face each day with faith, even when the way forward is not visible. Guide my steps and help me make decisions confidently, trusting in Your wisdom and direction.

Holy Spirit, I invite You into this space of uncertainty. Fill me with Your peace, and give me wisdom and insight as I navigate the unknowns of tomorrow. Help me trust Your perfect timing and plan, knowing You are always with me, even in the darkest moments. Thank you, Lord, for Your unwavering presence and promise to never leave or forsake me. I lean on Your strength and find solace in Your unending love.

In Jesus' name, I pray. Amen.

PRAYER FOR
Miraculous Intervention and Healing

"Heal me, Lord, and I will be healed; save me and I will be saved, for you are the one I praise."

JEREMIAH 17:14 (NIV)

"Praise the Lord, my soul, and forget not all his benefits—who forgives all your sins and heals all your diseases."

PSALM 103:2-3 (NIV)

Dear God,

I come before You with a heart full of desperation, asking for Your miraculous healing in my life. I need Your supernatural power! Heal me! I need Your healing touch more than ever. I ask that Your Holy Spirit fill me with strength and power, flowing through every part of me. Please, Lord, bring healing to my body, mind, spirit, and soul. I cry out to You, knowing You are the only one who can bring complete healing and restoration.

You are the God who works wonders and performs miracles. I praise You for Your healing power! I believe in Your boundless love and mighty power to bring healing into my life. Your compassion and strength know no bounds, and I trust Your ability to heal me from the top of my head to the soles of my feet. Touch every part of me that is affected by sickness or disease. Let Your healing power wash over me, restoring what has been damaged and bringing new life where there has been pain and suffering.

Increase my faith, Lord, even when doubt tries to creep in. I long to see Your miraculous work in my life, and I trust Your perfect plan.

Move in power, Holy Spirit, and heal me completely. I know that the God who created me has the power to heal me, and I praise Him for this! Let Your healing power shine through me, not only for my own relief but also as a testimony to others. I completely surrender to You, trusting Your healing touch and unending grace. Let Your light shine through my life, bringing glory to Your name and drawing others closer to You. Thank You, Lord, for Your unfailing love and the hope that You bring.

In Jesus' name, I pray. Amen.

Bible Versions Used

New International Version (NIV)
Holy Bible, New International Version®, NIV®. Copyright ©1973, 1978, 1984, 2011 by Biblica, Inc.® Used by permission.
All rights reserved worldwide.

New Revised Standard Version (NRSV)
Copyright © 1989 National Council of the Churches of Christ in the United States of America. Used by permission.
All rights reserved worldwide.

English Standard Version (ESV)
The Holy Bible, English Standard Version. ESV® Text Edition: 2016. Copyright © 2001 by Crossway Bibles, a publishing ministry of Good News Publishers.

For more Rescue Prayers